Pennsylvania Advance Medical Directives

A licensed Pennsylvania Attorney Explains how to Prepare your own Pennsylvania Advance Medical Directive Without a Lawyer.

About the Author

Robert P. Gasparro is an Elder Law Attorney with an office located in Haverford, Pennsylvania. He has drafted Advance Medical Directives for decades under both the old law and the 2007 revisions to the law. In addition to serving as an Elder Law attorney, he has served on the board of a nonprofit nursing and personal care home located in Philadelphia, Pennsylvania. In that capacity, he had an opportunity to see the results of the best and worst of Advance Healthcare Directives. He also teaches part of the DHS mandated course for individuals who seek a license to operate a personal care home in Pennsylvania.

Overview

This book is about a legal document known as an "Advance Health Care Directive." The document has two objectives: First, it will place someone in charge of making medical decisions for you if you are incapacitated. Second, the document will allow you to express your wishes about "end-of-life" care.

We will also prepare one of these documents as we go through this book. There are dozens of different documents in circulation purporting to be Advance Health Care Directives, but the Pennsylvania statute that governs the document contains its own form, which we will prepare in this course. The advantage of this form is that it has withstood the test of litigation since it was first introduced in 2007, and is recognized by many attorneys, judges and health care workers. The form was designed with input from lawyers, doctors, judges, and a committee who researched the law in other states.

Before we continue any further, please take a quick look at the sample document placed at the very end of this book. Note that it contains three parts. "Part I" is an explanation of the form and the law presented in non-technical language. It skillfully condenses the basics of about 84 statutes that regulate the legal document, most of which will be covered in this book. Beginning on line 115, we come across "Part II" which is called a Durable Health Care Power of Attorney. On lines 160-202, you have an opportunity to name your Health Care Agent and any alternatives if the first named agent is not available. On lines 205-234, you may describe some of your health care goals in your own words. On line 235, we see "Part III" of the document. This contains health care treatment instructions in the event of an end-stage medical condition or permanent unconsciousness. It also has the term "Living Will" in parenthesis. Following that, we see some choices about specific medical treatment options on lines 252-283. Next we see an organ donation option on lines 309-318, and a place to sign the form. This book will discuss these sections in depth, but a quick review of the form may help you see where everything fits in.

Important Terms:

Before we may continue, we must study some definitions. As you can see by the form we just examined, an Advance Health Care Directive has two parts. The first part is the" Durable Health Care Power of Attorney," and it is used whenever you are incompetent due to a medical condition that is expected to improve at some time. The second part, the "Living Will" is to take effect when your condition will not improve, and you have an end-stage medical condition or you are permanently unconscious. "End-Stage Medical Condition" means that you suffer from an incurable and irreversible medical condition that, in the opinion of the attending physician, is likely to result in death, despite medical treatment of any kind. "Permanent unconsciousness" means a condition such as an irreversible coma.

We sometimes hear of patients who recover from a coma after a long period, but that is the exception rather than the rule.

Some people in a coma may have a brief period of consciousness, but then revert to the original condition. The medical community has a good idea of what is, and what is not, "permanent unconsciousness." No matter what your medical condition, it is likely millions of people have had the same condition before you, with a predictable outcome.

Another term we will use is "principal" or "patient" to denote the person who prepares and signs one of these documents. I prefer the term "patient" and use it throughout this book.

We call a person appointed and serving under an Advance Medical Directive a "health care agent" or simply "agent." If a patient does not have an Advance Health Care Directive, the person who steps forward to make decisions is called a "health care representative" rather than a "health care agent."

We must also define "competency" in terms of this document, because most provisions of the document take over when a patient is "incompetent." There are different definitions of "competency" for different legal documents, but the people who drafted this set of laws provided a definition for us to use here. To determine if a patient is competent, one must ask three questions: First, is the patient able to understand the potential material benefits, risks and alternatives involved with a specific proposed health care decision? If so, is the patient able to make a decision on his or her own? If so, can the patient communicate that decision to others? If one or more of these are lacking, the patient is "incompetent." The statutes provide that anyone who presents a choice to a patient must also provide that patient with appropriate medical information, technical assistance to help them do research if necessary, and they must provide communication supportsto the patient if necessary. Therefore, they may need to implement a device that helps the patient hear or speak. The law specifically states that it is also known and expected that a patient may be able to make some decisions, but not others. Also, a patient's competency may come and go depending on time of day, a reaction to medication, or other factors. The patient should be allowed to make his or her own choice whenever possible, even if that means meeting with the patient when he or she is most likely to be competent. If the patient is not able to make a decision, only then does a "health care agent" or "health care representative" make decisions.

In Pennsylvania, Who Makes Decisions for an Incapacitated Person?

We have just introduced a new term above: "health care representative" for those who do <u>not</u> have an Advance Healthcare Directive. Who may serve as a "health care representative" for the people – estimated to be two-thirds of the population – who do not have one of these documents? Pennsylvania law provides a hierarchy. Just as the Pennsylvania laws determine how your estate is distributed if you do not have a Will, they determine who makes medical choices for you if you do not have an Advance Healthcare Directive. Unfortunately, many in the medical community do not understand this hierarchy. This author conducted an informal survey of nurses, hospital staff, nurse practitioners, and physicians, and fewer than 20% were able to explain the hierarchy of who makes decisions for a patient who does not have an Advance Medical Directive. Most health care workers try to obtain a consensus from the entire family about the patient's care, yet that is not what the drafters of the law wanted. Instead, they established a hierarchy, which is:

1. The spouse, unless an action for divorce has already been filed. If there is an adult child who is a child of the patient but not a child of the current spouse, each such child receives one vote along with the spouse. If there is a tie, the health care providers continue to administer health care treatment in accordance with accepted standards of medical practice until the disagreement is resolved.

2. If the patient has no spouse, then every adult child of the patient, including adopted children, have one vote. Ties are broken as above.

3. If the patient has no spouse or children, each adult brother or sister have one vote and ties are broken as above.

4. If the patient has no living spouse, children, brothers or sisters, then any adult grandchild has one vote and ties are broken as above.

5. If the patient has no surviving relatives, then any adult individual who is familiar with the patient's preferences and values and religious and moral beliefs, and who can assess how the patient would make health care decisions, may step forward.

The statute specifically says that if someone lower on the hierarchy has a closer relationship to the patient than another above them, they may petition a court to either disqualify an individual, or appoint them as the health care representative. This may happen, for example, if a patient is engaged but not married, or lives with someone they have not married. The disadvantage of this process, is that to be appointed the person must file a petition in court, and that may cost hundreds or thousands of dollars depending on the level opposition from others.

Another factor that complicates decision making for a person without an Advance Medical Directive is that the law states a "health care representative" must be reasonably available to make decisions, and if not, the person next in line makes the decisions. And when the person with higher priority becomes "reasonably available" again, they may resume duties. A flaw of the legislation is there may be no continuity in decision making for a patient who does not have an Advance Healthcare Directive.

Also, the person who assumes the duty of health care representative is obligated to let others in the hierarchy know that they have assumed those duties. They do not need to keep them updated on the patient's medical condition, just to let them know that they are acting as the "health care representative."

Finally, a health care representative is more limited in choices involving end-of-life care. Most would agree that it is much easier to complete an Advance Medical Directive than have to deal with all those variables presented above. Remember, the variables and conditions above only apply to someone who has not drafted an Advance Medical Directive.

What Kind of Decisions May An Agent or Healthcare Representative Make?

To understand what decisions that are permitted using one of these documents, one must understand some of the background about Advance Medical Directive laws. Prior to the 1950's, doctors and medical providers were obligated to do everything possible to keep patients alive. States later began to enact laws, and courts began to hand down decisions, allowing a patient to decline medical treatment. Although there was no Pennsylvania statute at the time, a court in Philadelphia recognized the right of Pennsylvania residents to decline medical treatment. Eventually, because the laws of the states differed, the United States Supreme Court recognized the right of a patient to decide what treatment they wanted, as well as any treatment they wished to decline, as a Constitutional Right. Accordingly, any adult has an absolute right to decline medical treatment. So long as a citizen is age 18 or over, he or she has a right to refuse blood transfusions, CPR, decline an ambulance ride to a hospital, or forego any other medical treatment. One also has a right to take morphine under prescription to relieve pain, even though it is likely to cause heart failure after prolonged use. However, one does not have the right to ask another's assistance to end their life. One may not ask another to administer an overdose of morphine, or any other drug, whose only goal is to cause death. That is criminal homicide. A patient or an agent under an advance medical directive may direct medical workers to discontinue any medical procedures. The powers of a "health care representative" on the other hand, may be more limited..

Duties and Rights of the Health Care Agent:

Due Diligence Duties of the Health Care Agent

It is this author's opinion that most people do not have an Advance Health Care Directive because they approach the task of drafting one the wrong way. People inspect the form and naturally try to focus on decisions about whether they want CPR, chemotherapy, a ventilator, feeding tubes or antibiotics. Many people do not know what a ventilator or chemotherapy accomplishes, let alone how it works. Second, most people cannot predict today what medical procedures they may want later. Even if one is in the final stages of cancer, and can only expect to live a few days, he or she may want a ventilator or feeding tube if it helps reduce stress. Also, a terminally ill patient in a nursing home who cuts his or her hand on a piece of furniture may not want the staff allow them bleed to death rather than have the wound treated. Our desire for medical treatment depends on circumstances we cannot predict, and the checkboxes next to each medical alternative become a moving target.

The more important matter, is that a patient designate who they want to be their health care agent. The Pennsylvania form allows a patient to appoint someone, and to give that person the ability to make a final decision, even if it sometimes means overriding the initial selections in the document made by the patient. Again, there is a provision in the document that allows a patient to say the instructions are "advisory only" and that the agent can override them if that is what is best. It is my experience that if a patient indicates general preferences, their agent will comply as appropriate under the circumstances. I advise checking off the appropriate boxes, but also making those choices advisory only, as you may do in lines 289-291 of the form.

An agent under one of these documents is a fiduciary, and as such, must exercise "due diligence." There are several parts of the law which regulate what an agent must do in order to comply with "due diligence." Unfortunately, not many agents are aware of these provisions, and neither are patients aware of the due diligence provisions when they appoint an agent. For the record, few health care workers are aware of the due diligence provisions either. But we will present them here in the hope that everyone will eventually comply with the law.

The due diligence requirements of an agent depend upon whether the patient is competent. Also, whether the decision involves routine medical care, surgery, or whether the decision involves end of life care.

<u>Duties of agent during competency determination:</u>

Since an agent has a fiduciary duty, he or she must read the Advance Medical Directive in its entirety, and if possible, engage in a conversation with the patient about the options and choices. The agent must make certain every effort is made to facilitate communication between the patient and medical staff so the patient can make the decision, even if it means that the agent collects information from the Internet or books for the patient to read. The agent might even read this information out loud to the patient. Also, most Advance Medical Directive forms, including the Pennsylvania form, allow the agent immediate access to medical records, whether or not the patient is incompetent. An agent might obtain copies of medical records and with the patient's permission, obtain a second opinion. One of the most beneficial things an agent may do is to review medical records for a patient living at a long term care facility who is about to transfer to or from a hospital. For example, a patient may be a resident of a nursing home, but something happens which requires a short stay at a hospital before returning to the nursing home again. First the agent can make certain the hospital staff have access to medical records from the nursing home, even if it means carrying copies to the hospital. Most likely the nursing home will send the records with the patient, but it does not hurt to check. Next, the agent can check the medication records after the patient returns from the hospital, to make certain all the medications are resumed the same as before the trip to the hospital, unless the hospital recommended a change in medications. If the hospital did recommend new medications, the agent could make sure those orders are known by the staff of the long term facility. There may also be confusion whether the hospital prescribed a new medication as a substitute for an old one, or in addition to the old one, and whether old medications should be renewed. The agent can clear up any confusion by getting the answers. This can be done even if the patient is "competent."

The next stage of an agent's duties occurs after a patient is deemed incompetent. In that case, the law specifically directs that the agent has all the same rights that the patient does, including the right to move to another facility if the agent feels that is what the patient would want. The agent should make the decision that the patient would make if competent. Conversely, the statute specifically says that an agent must keep the patient's health information private, except as necessary to aid in treatment. An agent may not indiscriminately discuss the patient's medical condition with strangers, or on Facebook. And never include pictures of the patient in any Facebook posting unless they are able to consent.

After Incompetency Determination -Agent's duties toward routine medical decisions:

After the patient is determined to be incompetent as defined by the statute, it specifically states that in regard to any routine medical decision, an agent must: (1) Obtain all relevant medical information.(2) Make a decision based on the following criteria, in this order of priority: a) The decision must be made in accordance with any clear written or verbal instructions the patient has given to the agent; b) If there are no such instructions, the decision must be made in conformity with the patient's general preferences and values, including the patient's religious or moral belief; c) If none of the aforementioned exist, the decision must be in the patient's best interest, as determined by the agent.

After Incompetency Determination - Agent's duties toward surgery, administration of anesthesia, radiation, chemotherapy, blood transfusion, insertion of a surgical device or appliance, the use of any experimental medication or device or use of an approved medication or device in an experimental manner:

If the patient is incompetent, the statute specifically states, that if faced with a decision enumerated above, the health care agent must, in addition to the procedures for routine care: (1) Gather information about the patient's prognoses and acceptable alternatives for the diagnoses, treatment and supportive care for the illness. (2) Speak to the patient's doctor about the risks and alternatives of each medical treatment, as well as understand the process involved in each treatment. The physician is obligated to give the agent all the information required by Section 504 of the Medical Care Availability and Reduction of Error Act. In most cases that simply means enough information to allow a decision after informed consent. (3) Although optional, the statute suggests that the agent might want to research the credentials of the doctor performing the surgery. After completing the foregoing steps, the agent may consent to, or decline any proposed care if the agent in good faith feels that the patient would do so because of personal choice, or moral or religious beliefs.

After Incompetency Determination - Agent's duty toward "end of life" decisions.

If an agent must make a decision involving end-of-life care for an incompetent patient, they must, in addition to the foregoing, take additional steps. The agent must distinguish between the current condition which is likely to cause death, and any other concurrent disease, illness or physical, mental, cognitive or intellectual condition of the patient. The agent must generally continue to treat the other conditions. So if a patient who receives Metformin to control diabetes is also dying of cancer, the agent should make certain the patient continues to receive the Metformin. Next, if the patient is in an "end-stage medical condition" the agent must distinguish between palliative and curative care. Palliative care is that which makes someone more comfortable, and it should be initiated or continued. For example, an agent may call for Hospice Care even if the patient is in a nursing home. The nursing home may provide some recommendations for hospice care, but the hospice agency will provide care beyond that provided by the nursing home.

If the principal has left instructions regarding end of life care, the agent must consult them. The agent must follow the instructions unless given discretion to deviate from them in appropriate circumstances. If the agent has not received any instructions about end of life care, the agent must make end of life decisions that he or she feels conforms to the patient's preferences and values and morals and religious beliefs. In the very rare case where the agent does not know any of the foregoing, then the agent must make a decision that is in the patient's best interest considering, first- the preservation of life, then the relief from suffering, and last, the preservation or restoration of functioning. Although we mention them here, if the patient has already filled out an advance medical directive, the agent should rarely ever have to make these considerations.

Regarding end-of-life decisions, the Pennsylvania statute was enacted just two years after a famous New Jersey case that dealt with a feeding tube. The legislature wanted a separate paragraph placed in our Advance Medical Directive form, on whether or not a patient wanted a feeding tube inserted if they were in an "end stage medical condition." My experience is that most check off the box that says they do not want a feeding tube. However, some, for religious reasons, state that they want the feeding tube inserted. There is no right answer, it is a matter of personal choice.

Rights of the Health Care Agent:

The statute specifically directs the Pennsylvania Dept. of Health to implement procedures to insure that every health care provider in the state has a system of policies and procedures to help the agent go through the process we just covered.

The statute also states that any health care agent, who incurs reasonable expenses not covered by insurance, including the purchase of health care insurance itself, is entitled to reimbursement from the patient's agent under a financial Power of Attorney, or from their guardian.

The statute empowers the agent under a health care directive to arrange the disposition of the patient's body, and to make anatomical gifts.

How to Execute the Advance Health Care Directive:

Please proceed to the form that is provided in the package. This is the sample form provided in the statute.

If you have a form from a different state that was valid in that state when executed, it will be recognized as valid in Pennsylvania. However, that may involve contacting an attorney in the other state to assure the form is valid there. It may be easier to simply execute a new Pennsylvania form.

You will notice this form is broken down into three sections. The first part lines 1-114, is a very good synopsis of the law relating to this document. Most will generally keep the explanation as part of the form, so that any third party who reads the document can understand it better.

Then on line 115, we have Part II which is the Durable Health Care Power of Attorney. Remember, this is the part of the form that directs your agent if you are incapacitated, but may yet recover or stabilize at some time in the future. The first paragraph of this section, lines 122-135, gives your agent an immediate right to receive a copy or inspect your medical records. We already explained that you may be competent, but it would be difficult for you to get these records in order to get a "second opinion" Or, your agent may want to transport records to and from a long term care facility to a hospital. There is a statutory fee for obtaining copies of some medical records, but it is not prohibitive. On line 136, the document states that the rest of the document is effective only when you are incompetent, as we defined that condition earlier. It also says that your agent may not delegate the power to make decisions. If your agent cannot make decisions for you, they must let the successor agent in your document take over. This often happens if you name your spouse as your agent when you draft the document, but later your spouse is also incapacitated and unable to serve. In that case your successor agent steps in.

Next, the document gives your health care agent six specific powers on lines 141-158. If for any reason you do not want to give your health care agent one of the six powers, strike it out. The overwhelming majority of people just leave the paragraphs as they stand, without striking out anything, but it is a matter of personal choice.

Next in lines 160-204, you appoint your health care agent, and an alternative agent in case the first cannot serve. You should list two alternatives if you can, but not everyone can. One important caveat: you may not name one of your health care workers as your agent unless they are also related to you by blood, marriage or adoption. You may not name your nurse or anyone at the nursing home or other facility as your agent, unless they are related to you as above. Also, both you and your agent must generally be at least 18 years old. Remember this point if you try to make one of these forms for one of your minor children, or if you try to make one of your minor children your agent. You cannot do that unless the minor is also a high school graduate, married, or legally emancipated. For purposes of these laws only, anyone under age 18 who is a high school graduate, married, or legally emancipated is considered an adult.

In this author's experience, it is important to appoint an agent who lives close and who can visit you every day, or every few days. Although you may have a son or daughter who is a doctor in a distant state, it is more important that your agent can make certain your bed is comfortable, that you have something to occupy your time, and that your room is always clean and cheery.

Your agent can be encouraged to consult with the son or daughter who is a nurse or doctor, and your children can come to visit you few weeks, but if possible, appoint someone who lives near you your agent.

After you appoint your primary and successor agents, we come to a section in lines 207-218 where you list your goals in order to guide your agent. Many people state their goal is to be comfortable and free of pain. Others feel that, in order to preserve the dignity of life, they want to be kept as conscious as possible whether or not they must endure pain. Some have specifically stated they wanted to be used for research to the extent it was medically ethical and possible. Many people also leave that section entirely blank. It is a matter of personal choice and there is no correct answer.

On lines 219-233 we come to an important provision about irreversible brain damage or brain disease with no realistic hope of significant recovery. This can be a slippery slope, but it is a very important paragraph. Under this paragraph, if a person has irreversible brain damage or brain disease which will not cause death, the document directs medical care workers to provide medical treatment to them just as though they had an end stage medical condition. How does this work? This author had a friend who slipped in a supermarket and something went wrong during surgery related to that accident. The operation caused significant brain damage. Although she was a bright person before the surgery, the patient had the abilities and maturity of a 5th grade child following the surgery. Would her family render CPR to her if she needed it? The answer is that they certainly would! Although she had significant and irreversible brain damage, they still enjoyed her company. What about those who suffer from Parkinson's Disease? Unlike Alzheimer's, Parkinson's disease is not fatal. Indeed, Michael Fox, who was afflicted with Parkinson's, entertained us for decades with television shows. Some working professionals are afflicted with Parkinson's but still serve as important citizens and neighbors.

However the health of both those enumerated above decline, and the quality of life may also decline after some time. Under those circumstances, a person with severe Parkinson's or irreversible brain damage may want to decline CPR. The question is, at what stage of the disease would they begin to think that way. Despite the ethical dilemma, nearly every client seems to check that box that says that if they have severe and irreversible brain damage, they want to be treated like someone with an end-stage medical condition or permanent unconsciousness. As stated earlier, a patient does not have a right to assisted suicide, but they do have a right to decline medical care at any stage of their life, and that is what this paragraph attempts to accomplish.

Most of us want to live out our life without fear that our agent will allow us to die simply because we are not at full capacity. Luckily, there is a saving provision that we will review later, which makes all of your directions advisory only, and gives an agent the ability to override anything checked off. Most individuals are uncertain how they will die, and are loath to direct medical care for conditions they cannot predict. Therefore, we will check off the box on lines 284-291 that says the instructions are advisory only.

On line 235, we begin the Living Will. This is the part of the document that directs medical care in the event of an end-stage medical condition that will result in death despite any medical treatment, or for someone permanently unconscious or in an irreversible vegetative state with no hope of recovery.

There are three choices about medical care in the document, with the opportunity to strike out one or more choices. The first set of choices is in lines 253-270. Most people just leave them blank and do not strike out any paragraph. However, it is a matter of personal preference and there is no right answer.

On lines 271-282 is a separate paragraph asking if you want a feeding tube if you are at an end-stage medical condition or permanently unconscious. This procedure gets its own separate paragraph because at the time the law was being drafted there was a well-publicized N.J. case that dealt with use of a feeding tube to preserve life. Most say they do not want a feeding tube, although it is a matter of personal preference.

And finally, on lines 284-291, is the most important paragraph of the entire document. This author strongly suggests that you chose the second option and state to your agent that "These instructions are only for guidance and your agent shall have final say and may override any of your instructions"

Then lines 298-307 contain boilerplate to protect the agent so long as he or she acts in good faith.

Page 309-318 give you an opportunity to opt for organ donation, or not. Many people leave this blank knowing that they can make these designations for organ donation or vascularized composite allografts donations in their driver's license. However it is a matter of personal choice.

Finally, please date and sign the document on lines 323-329. If you cannot sign yourself, as often happens when someone is bedridden or in a cast, then someone may sign for you. However, the person who signs for you may not be one of your health care workers. Nor may any person who signed for you be a witness. You must be of "sound mind" to sign this document, but the statute does not define sound mind. Most people are presumed to be of sound mind, so the burden of proof is on anyone who wants to contest the document. If you have the energy, you may also initial the bottom of each page. Although it is not required, it is good practice.

Lines 332-338, the form asks for two witnesses who are at least 18 years old. The witnesses may be employees of the health care facility where you are staying, or anyone else. Although the form does not ask for it, it may be a good idea to get the address of the witness in case it becomes an issue later whether the patient was of sound mind to sign the document. A business address is sufficient.

Finally, on lines 346-366, you have an opportunity to have the document notarized. The witnesses do not need to be present when the document is notarized. Notarization is always a good idea.

If you ever wish to revoke this document, you may simply rip it up. If you are competent, you may also revoke it by telling your health care workers that you want to revoke it, or by sending a written note to them. If you are of sound mind, you can revoke a Medical Power of Attorney at any time.

With regard to the Living Will, you may, at any time, change your mind and tell your health care workers that you wish to be kept alive. You may do this despite what you have previously written or directed. In fact, according to the laws, you do not even need to be of sound mind to make this decision to be kept alive.

Commonwealth of Pennsylvania Rights and Duties:

The preamble to this document mentions that the state also has rights if the patient is a pregnant woman. Health care workers do not have an obligation to perform a pregnancy test unless they have reason to believe a patient is pregnant. If a woman is found to be pregnant, health care workers are obligated to provide life-sustaining treatment, nutrition and hydration, despite any other directions in your Advance Health Care Directive. There is an exception, however, if both the attending physician and an obstetrician who has examined the woman both agree that: (1) They could not maintain the woman in such a way as to permit the continued development and live birth of the unborn child, or (2) Providing the aforementioned treatment would be physically harmful to the pregnant woman, or (3) Providing the aforementioned treatment would cause pain to the pregnant woman that could not be alleviated by medication. If a health care worker does keep a woman alive pursuant to this section, the Commonwealth of Pennsylvania will pay the costs not covered by insurance, and will not seek reimbursement from the pregnant woman's estate or anyone else.

The state also has an obligation to prevent homicide, so this body of laws contains criminal penalties for anyone who conceals, forges or modifies an Advance Health Care Directive without authorization. Penalties are also provided for anyone who willfully conceals or withholds information that one of these documents exists, or has been revoked. Finally, there are criminal penalties imposed against anyone who uses undue influence, fraud or duress to compel a patient to execute of these documents.

Health Care Provider Rights and Duties:

Duties of Health Care Providers

The most important duty for a health care worker is to read the document! We read in the news that these documents are sometimes ignored by hospitals and doctors. That may be because no doctor or nurse wants to try to decipher a legal document. The problem is further compounded by the fact that there is no cause of action for "wrongful life" although one may be sued for "wrongful death." The solution for this problem is a proactive agent. This is very important. The agent under the Advance Health Care Directive should provide a copy of the document and tell the patient's medical staff that he or she is available to answer any of their questions about the document. It is also helpful if the agent examines the medical records of the patient every few visits to make certain they are legible, and that all of the prescribed medications and/or doctor's orders are being administered.

While the body of laws specifically suggests that the attending physician discuss a Living Will when a patient develops an end-stage medical condition, or upon admission to a health care facility, the law says that if a patient does not have an Advance Health care Directive, health care workers cannot make any presumptions about what kind of care the patient might want.

Also, a health care provider or insurance company may not require a customer to complete an Advance Health Care Directive in order to receive services or insurance. Neither may they charge a different rate based upon whether or not a customer has an

Advance Health Care Directive. Finally, a health care worker may not designate or disqualify a person to act as a health care agent as a condition of providing services to a patient.

<u>Duties and rights imposed on attending physician:</u>

The law imposes several duties on the attending physician. The agent under an Advance Health Care Directive may take steps to insure they are followed. First, the attending physician must actually read the document. Also, any determination that the patient is incompetent must be entered in the patient's medical records. Any revocation of a Living Will must also be memorialized in the patient's medical records. If the patient enters into an end-stage medical condition or becomes permanently unconscious, the attending physician must promptly certify that status in writing. In that case, the law encourages, but does not require, that the attending physician have a discussion with the patient about end of life issues. If the discussion does take place, however, it must be documented in the medical record. Finally, the law states that whenever possible, any decisions made by a health care agent should also be communicated to the patient. Understandably, in most cases, since the patient will be incompetent, this may not be feasible. In some cases, however, such as helping the patient obtain medical records or a second opinion, this section would come into play.

<u>Rights of Health Care Providers.</u>

So long as they have read the patient's Advance Health Care Directive, the physician or health care provider has the right to require a written declaration from any person who asserts the authority to act as a health care agent or representative, that they have the power. The writing must indicate the facts and circumstances sufficient to prove the authority. This section of the law generally comes into play when a "health care representative" asserts that he or she has the authority to step forward on behalf of a patient who does not have an Advance Healthcare Directive.

If the attending physician or other health care provider cannot in good conscience comply with a decision of a health care agent or the patient, they are not obligated to perform those procedures. However, they must inform the patient or the patient's agent, and make every reasonable effort to assist in the transfer of the patient to another physician or health care provider who will comply with the wishes. If no other facility can be found, or if the patient refuses to move, they may ignore the decisions of the patient or agent, and treat according to their moral imperatives.

Any health care worker, or any employee or staff member of a health care provider may not be forced to participate if a decision of a patient is against their religious convictions or morals. They may not be required to participate in the withholding or withdrawal of life sustaining treatment if they do not agree with it. In that case, they must inform their employer in writing of their choice not to participate. If they do so, the law protects them by stating that their employer may not discharge them, or in any manner discriminate against them because of their beliefs.

Finally, the law specifically states the following rights and obligations of health care providers:

A health care worker may not be subject to criminal or civil liability, discipline for unprofessional conduct, administrative sanctions, and may not be found to have committed an act of unprofessional conduct if they do any of the following: (1) If they participate in not giving life-sustaining treatment or CPR to a patient so long as the health care worker believes in good faith that he or she is following the patient's wishes under these laws; (2) If they comply with any direction of the health care agent which does not contradict the terms of the written Advance Health Care Directive; (3) If they refuse to comply with any direction from a health care agent or representative who is not acting in accordance with their duties of due diligence, or if they have a good faith belief the person does not have authority; (4) If there is no agent, the health care provider must comply with the written directions of that document so long as they believe it is valid. (5) A health care worker cannot be punished for disclosing health care information to someone who they believe in good faith to be the agent, even if it turns out later the person had no such authority; (6) A heath care worker is free to refuse to comply with the wishes of a document or an agent if they believe that following the directions would be unethical in that the proposed action would result in medical care that, to a reasonable degree of medical certainty, would have no medical basis in addressing a need or condition of the patient.

Conclusion

We have covered a significant number of rules in our discussion of Advance Healthcare Directives. The laws in Pennsylvania are somewhat unique compared to other jurisdictions in that they provide more detail and guidance than many other states. We did not cover POLST documents. It is this author's belief that having a good agent under and Advance Healthcare Directive is superior to drafting a POLST document because the Agent can make certain that the Advance Healthcare Directive becomes part of the patient's medical record, and the agent is given flexibility on healthcare options, depending upon the circumstances. Also, the Advance Healthcare Directive covers many more issues than a POLST including the option to arrange for disposition of the body after death, the option to arrange for a transfer of the patient to another facility if that would be beneficial, the option to obtain a second opinion, and other features covered in this book. Most important, the option to make a final decision dependent upon the circumstances that could not be predicted when the document was drafted.

Still confused? Want more?

Although this book is designed to allow you to complete your own document without anything more, if you would like more information, you may watch a video of this presentation, download materials, and while you prepare your document, you may consult with an attorney and/or nurse practitioner to answer your questions. Follow the link below for this option.

<u>Online Advance Medical Directive</u>

Or if you prefer to have a an office consultation for the basic estate planning documents including this Advance Medical Directive, a simple Will, a Financial Power of Attorney, a Standby Guardianship for a Minor Child, follow the link below.

<u>Office consultation</u>

Copyright © 2019 Robert P. Gasparro
All rights reserved

Pennsylvania Advance Medical Directive Document begins on next page.

DURABLE HEALTH CARE POWER OF ATTORNEY AND HEALTH CARE TREATMENT INSTRUCTIONS
(LIVING WILL)
PART I   INTRODUCTORY REMARKS ON HEALTH CARE DECISION MAKING

You have the right to decide the type of health care you want. Should you become unable to understand, make or communicate decisions about medical care, your wishes for medical treatment are most likely to be followed if you express those wishes in advance by: (1) naming a health care agent to decide treatment for you; and (2) giving health care treatment instructions to your health care agent or health care provider. An advance health care directive is a written set of instructions expressing your wishes for medical treatment. It may contain a health care power of attorney, where you name a person called a "health care agent" to decide treatment for you, and a living will, where you tell your health care agent initiation, continuation, withholding or withdrawal of life-sustaining treatment and other specific directions.

You may limit your health care agent's involvement in deciding your medical treatment so that your health care agent will speak for you only when you are unable to speak for yourself or you may give your health care agent the power to speak for you immediately. This combined form gives your health care agent the power to speak for you only when you are unable to speak for yourself. A living will cannot be followed unless your attending physician determines that you lack the ability to understand, make or communicate health care decisions for yourself and you are either permanently unconscious or you have an end-stage medical condition, which is a condition that will result in death despite the introduction or continuation of medical treatment. You, and not your health care agent, remain responsible for the cost of your medical care.

If you do not write down your wishes about your health care in advance, and if later you become unable to understand, make or communicate these decisions, those wishes may not be honored because they may remain unknown to others.

A health care provider who refuses to honor your wishes about health care must tell you of its refusal and help to transfer you to a health care provider who will honor your wishes.

You should give a copy of your advance health care directive (a living will, health care power of attorney or a document containing both) to your health care agent, your physicians, family members and others whom you expect would likely attend to your needs if you become unable to understand, make or communicate decisions about medical care. If your health care wishes change, tell your physician and write a new advance health care directive to replace your old one. It is important in selecting a health care agent that you choose a person you trust who is likely to be available in a medical situation where you cannot make decisions for yourself. You should inform that person that you have appointed him or her so that your health care agent will understand your health care objectives.

You may wish to consult with knowledgeable, trusted individuals such as family members, your physician or clergy when considering an expression of your values and health care wishes. You are free to create your own advance health care directive to convey your wishes regarding medical treatment. The following form is an example of an advance health care directive that combines a health care power of attorney with a living will.

NOTES ABOUT THE USE OF THIS FORM

If you decide to use this form or create your own advance health care directive, you should consult with your physician and your attorney to make sure that your wishes are clearly expressed and comply with the law. If you decide to use this form but disagree with any of its statements, you may cross out those statements. You may add comments to this form or use your own form to help your physician or health care agent decide your medical care.

This form is designed to give your health care agent broad powers to make health care decisions for you whenever you cannot make them for yourself. It is also designed to express a desire to limit or authorize care if you have an end-stage medical condition or are permanently unconscious. If you do not desire to give your health care agent broad powers, or you know not wish to limit your care if you have an end-stage medical condition or are permanently unconscious, you may wish to use a different form or create your own. You should also use a different form if you wish to express your preferences in more detail than this form allows or if you wish for your health care agent to be able to speak for you immediately. In these situations, it is particularly important that you consult with your attorney and physician to make sure that your wishes are clearly expressed and that your form complies with the law.

This form allows you to tell your health care agent your goals if you have an end-stage medical condition or other extreme and irreversible medical condition, such as advanced Alzheimer's disease. Do you want medical care applied aggressively in these situations or would you consider such aggressive medical care burdensome and undesirable.

You may choose whether you want your health-care agent to be bound by your instructions or whether you want your health care agent to be able to decide at the time what course of treatment the health care agent thinks most fully reflects your wishes and values

If you are a woman and diagnosed as being pregnant at the time a health care decision would otherwise be made pursuant to this form, the laws of this Commonwealth prohibit implementation of that decision if it directs that life-sustaining treatment, including nutrition and hydration, be withheld or withdrawn from you, unless your attending physician and an obstetrician who have examined you certify in your medical record that the life-sustaining treatment: (1)

will not maintain you in such a way as to permit the continuing development and live birth of the unborn child; (2) will be physically harmful to you; or (3) will cause pain to you that cannot be alleviated by medication.

A physician is not required to perform a pregnancy test on you unless the physician has reason to believe that you are pregnant.

Pennsylvania law protects your health care agent and health care providers from any legal liability for following in good faith your wishes as expressed in the form or by your health care agent's direction. It does not otherwise change professional standards or excuse negligence in the way your wishes are carried out. If you have any questions about the law, consult an attorney for guidance.

This form and explanation is not intended to take the place of specific legal or medical advice for which you should rely upon your own attorney and physician.

PART II
DURABLE HEALTH CARE POWER OF ATTORNEY

I,_____, of _____ County, Pennsylvania, appoint the person named below to be my health care agent to make health and personal care decisions for me.

Effective immediately and continuously until my death or revocation by a writing signed by me or someone authorized to make health care treatment decisions for me, I authorize all health care providers or other covered entities to disclose to my health care agent, upon my agent's request, any information, oral or written, regarding my physical or mental health, including, but not limited to, medical and hospital records and what is otherwise private, privileged, protected or personal health information, such as health information as defined and described in the Health Insurance Portability and Accountability Act of 1996 (Public Law 104-191, 110 Stat. 1936), the regulations promulgated thereunder and any other State or local laws and rules. Information disclosed by a health care provider or other covered entity may be redisclosed and may no longer be subject to the privacy rules provided by 45 C.F.R. pt. 164.

The remainder of this document will take effect when and only when I lack the ability to understand, make or communicate a choice regarding a health or personal care decision as verified by my attending physician. My health care agent may not delegate the authority to make decisions.

My health care agent has all of the following powers subject to the health care treatment instructions that follow in part III. (Cross out any powers you do not want to give your health care agent:)

1. To authorize, withhold or withdraw medical care and surgical procedures.

2. To authorize, withhold or withdraw nutrition (food) or hydration (water) medically supplied by tube through my nose, stomach, intestines, arteries or veins.

3. To authorize my admission to or discharge from a medical, nursing, residential or similar facility and to make agreements for my care and health insurance for my care, including hospice and/or palliative care.

4. To hire and fire medical, social service and other support personnel responsible for my care.

5. To take any legal action necessary to do what I have directed.

6. To request that a physician responsible for my care issue a do-not-resuscitate (DNR) order, including an out-of hospital DNR order, and sign any required documents and consents.

APPOINTMENT OF HEALTH CARE AGENT

I appoint the following health care agent:

Health Care Agent:

(Name and relationship)

Address:

Telephone Number: Home   Work

E-Mail:

If you do not name a health care agent, health care providers will ask your family or an adult who knows your preferences and values for help in determining your wishes for treatment. Note that you may not appoint your doctor or other health care provider as your health care agent unless related to you by blood, marriage, or adoption.

If my health care agent is not readily available or if my health care agent is my spouse and an action for divorce is filed by either of us after the date of this document, I appoint the person or persons named below in the order named. (It is helpful,: but not required, to make alternative health care agents.)

First Alternative Health Care agent

(Name and relationship)

Address:

Telephone Number: Home: Work:
E-MAIL:

Second Alternative Health Care Agent: A

Agent

(Name and relationship)

Address:
Telephone Number: Home: Work:
E-MAIL:

GUIDANCE FOR HEALTH CARE AGENT (OPTIONAL)

GOALS

If I have an end-stage medical condition or other extreme irreversible medical condition, my goals in making medical decisions are as follows (insert your personal priorities in your own words, such as comfort, care, preservation of mental function, etc.):

SEVERE BRAIN DAMAGE OR BRAIN DISEASE

If I should suffer from severe and irreversible brain damage or brain disease with no realistic hope of significant recovery, I would consider such a condition intolerable and the application of aggressive medical care to be burdensome. I therefore request that my health care agent respond to any intervening (other and separate) life-threatening conditions in the same manner as directed for an end-stage medical condition or state of permanent unconsciousness and I have indicated below.

Initials ____ I agree   or

Initials ____ I disagree

PART III
HEALTH CARE TREATMENT INSTRUCTIONS IN THE EVENT OF END-STAGE MEDICAL CONDITION OR PERMANENT UNCONSCIOUSNESS

(LIVING WILL)

The following health care treatment instructions exercise my right to make my own health care decisions. These instructions are intended to provide clear and convincing evidence of my wishes to be followed when I lack the capacity to understand, make or communicate my treatment decisions:

If I have an end-stage medical condition (which will result in my death, despite the introduction or continuation of medical treatment) or am permanently unconscious such as an irreversible coma or an irreversible vegetative state and there is not realistic hope of significant recovery, all of the following apply (cross out any treatment instruction with which you do not agree) :

1. I direct that I be given health care treatment to relieve pain or provide comfort even if such treatment might shorten my life, suppress my appetite or my breathing, or be habit forming.

2. I direct that all life prolonging procedures be withheld or withdrawn.

3. I specifically do not want any of the following as life prolonging procedures: (If you wish to receive any of these treatments, write "I do want" after the treatment)

- Heart-lung resuscitation (CPR)
- Mechanical ventilator (breathing machine)
- Dialysis (kidney machine) Surgery
- Chemotherapy
- Radiation treatment
- Antibiotics

Please indicate whether you want nutrition (food) or hydration (water) medically supplied by a tube into your nose, stomach, intestine, arteries, or veins if you have an end-stage medical condition or are permanently unconscious and there is no realistic hope of significant recovery.

(Initial only one statement.)

TUBE FEEDINGS

_____I want tube feedings to be given

OR

NO TUBE FEEDINGS

_____I do not want tube feedings to be given.

HEALTH CARE AGENT'S USE OF INSTRUCTIONS

(INITIAL ONE OPTION ONLY)

_____My health care agent must follow these instructions

OR

_____These instructions are only guidance. My health care agent shall have final say and may override any of my instructions. (Indicate any exceptions)

If I did not appoint a health care agent, these instructions shall be followed.

LEGAL PROTECTION

Pennsylvania law protects my health care agent and health care providers from any legal liability for their good faith actions in following my wishes as expressed in this form or in complying with my health care agent's direction. On behalf of myself, my executors and heirs, I further hold my health care agent and my health care providers harmless and indemnify them against any claim for their good faith actions in recognizing my health care agent's authority or in following my treatment instructions.

ORGAN DONATION (INITIAL ONE OPTION ONLY)

_____I consent to donate my organs and tissues at the time of my death for the purpose of transplant, medical study or education.

{Insert any limitations you desire on donation of specific organs or tissues or uses for donation or organs and tissues.)

OR

_____-I do not consent to donate my organs or tissues at the time of my death.

SIGNATURE

Having carefully read this document, I have signed it this _____ day of _____ 20___, revoking all previous health care powers of attorney and health care treatment instructions.

_____

(Sign full name here for health care power of attorney and health care treatment instructions.)

WITNESS:_____
ADDRESS:_____

WITNESS:_____
ADDRESS:_____

Two witnesses at least 18 years of age are required by Pennsylvania law and should witness your signature in each other's presence. A person who signs this document on behalf of and at the direction of a principal may not be a witness. (It is preferable if the witnesses are not your heirs, nor your creditors, nor employed by any of your health care providers.)

NOTARIZATION (OPTIONAL)

(Notarization of document is not required by Pennsylvania law, by if the document is both witnessed and notarized, it is more likely to be honored by the laws of some other states.)

On this   day of   , 20 , before me personally appeared the aforesaid declarant and principal, _____and the witnesses _____and _____to me known to be the person described in and who executed the foregoing instrument and acknowledged that he/she executed the same as his/her free act and deed.

IN WITNESS WHEREOF, I have hereunto set my hand and affixed my official seal in the County of._____, State of_____ the day and year first above written.

363	_____
364	Notary Public
365	_____
366	My commission expires

www.ingramcontent.com/pod-product-compliance
Lightning Source LLC
Chambersburg PA
CBHW030738180526
45157CB00008BA/3228